HTML

QuickStart Guide

The Simplified Beginner's Guide To HTML

Martin Mihajlov
in partnership with

Copyright 2016 by ClydeBank Media - All Rights Reserved.

This document is geared towards providing exact and reliable information in regards to the topic and issue covered. The publication is sold with the idea that the publisher is not required to render accounting, officially permitted, or otherwise, qualified services. If advice is necessary, legal or professional, a practiced individual in the profession should be ordered.

From a Declaration of Principles which was accepted and approved equally by a Committee of the American Bar Association and a Committee of Publishers and Associations. In no way is it legal to reproduce, duplicate, or transmit any part of this document in either electronic means or in printed format. Recording of this publication is strictly prohibited and any storage of this document is not allowed unless with written permission from the publisher.

The information provided herein is stated to be truthful and consistent, in that any liability, in terms of inattention or otherwise, by any usage or abuse of any policies, processes, or directions contained within is the solitary and utter responsibility of the recipient reader. Under no circumstances will any legal responsibility or blame be held against the publisher for any reparation, damages, or monetary loss due to the information herein, either directly or indirectly. Respective authors own all copyrights not held by the publisher. The information herein is offered for informational purposes solely, and is universal as so. The presentation of the information is without contract or any type of guarantee assurance.

Trademarks: All trademarks are the property of their respective owners. The trademarks that are used are without any consent, and the publication of the trademark is without permission or backing by the trademark owner. All trademarks and brands within this book are for clarifying purposes only and are owned by the owners themselves, not affiliated with this document.

ClydeBank Media LLC is not associated with any organization, product or service discussed in this book. The publisher has made every effort to ensure that the information presented in this book was accurate at time of publication. All precautions have been taken in the preparation of this book. The publisher, author, editor and designer assume no responsibility for any loss, damage, or disruption caused by errors or omissions from this book, whether such errors or omissions result from negligence, accident, or any other cause.

Edition # 1 – Updated : May 2, 2016

Cover Illustration and Design: Katie Poorman, Copyright © 2016 by ClydeBank Media LLC
Interior Design: Katie Poorman, Copyright © 2016 by ClydeBank Media LLC

ClydeBank Media LLC
P.O Box 6561
Albany, NY 12206
Printed in the United States of America

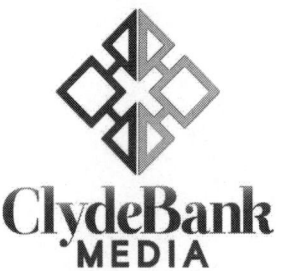

Copyright © 2016
ClydeBank Media LLC
www.clydebankmedia.com
All Rights Reserved

ISBN-13 : 978-1511617994

contents

1	INTRODUCTION	7
	HTML Terminology	7
	The Concept of Document Structure	10
	A Little Background	13
2	BASIC PAGE STRUCTURE	17
	Basic Document Template	17
	Additional Head Tags	19
	Document Declaration	21
3	PAGE CONTENT	23
	Paragraphs & Line Breaks	23
	Creating Headlines	25
	Lists	27
	Quotations	33
	Additional Text Elements	34
	Tables	40
	Special Characters	45
	HTML Comments	55
	Wrapping Things Up	57
4	CONTENT STRUCTURE	59
	Sectioning Content	59
	Headers & Footers	64
	Semantic Images with <figure> & <figcaption>	65
	HTML5 Compatibility	66
SUMMARY		73
GLOSSARY		75
ABOUT CLYDEBANK		77

Terms displayed in ***bold italic*** can be found defined in the glossary, starting on page 75.

&

Feel free to take notes beginning on page 78.

| 1 |
Introduction

Hypertext Markup Language, more commonly known as HTML, is the language of the World Wide Web (WWW). Knowing HTML is one of the core skills of any web designer and therefore should be one of the first things to master.

In this book, we will learn everything we need to know about HTML, from understanding HTML documents to writing fully HTML5-compliant web pages. First, we will focus on the basics of HTML syntax, tags and attributes, and learn the process of structuring documents. Next, we will study the most common HTML elements that make up the bulk of the language such as paragraphs, headings, lists and tables. Finally, we will look at the HTML5 sectioning elements designed to create more meaningful documents, which will in turn help us create pages with greater semantic meaning.

HTML Terminology

As mentioned previously, HTML is an acronym for Hypertext Markup Language. If we observe this full name more closely, it means *language for marking hyper text*, and "marking" is the operative word. Markup language refers to a plain text language that is not even remotely related with programming. The word "hyper" symbolizes the web tendencies of this language. When the concept was conceived ***"hypertext"*** was a buzzword that indicated the linking of documents.

Elements & Tags

Even though a web page we look at today may be full of text, pictures and videos, underneath that facade is a single long file full of HTML text. When we "ask" our browser for a web page, the browser retrieves a document written in HTML, a language our browser can understand and interpret. The text has "markings" that instruct the browser where things begin, where they end, and what purpose they serve.

To prepare a document for the web, we need to go through the simple process of marking up the text with a specific set of textual elements called tags. A ***tag*** is the basic building block of a ***web page*** and is essentially a reserved word placed between the '<' and '>' characters. For example, the element <html> represents a tag.

All tags in HTML come in pairs, meaning there is a tag that signals the beginning of the element, also known as an **opening tag**, and a tag that signals the end the element called a **closing tag**. The opening and the closing tags have the same name, with the only difference being that the name of the closing tag is always preceded by the slash character '/'.

For example, the following HTML code:

```
Carl<strong>Jung</strong>
```

will be displayed on the page as:
Carl **Jung**

NOTE

While marked up text has a default "look" in the browser, the actual visual representation of HTML elements is controlled by a different set of rules called *Cascading Style Sheets* (CSS).

When a web browser reads the HTML document and reaches the <strong> element, it doesn't display the text <strong> on the web page. Instead, when the browser encounters a tag, it interprets it as a command to display text in a specific, predefined way. In this example, when encountering the <strong> tag the browser interprets that from that point on the text is marked up as strong, more important text, and it displays that text in bold until it reaches the closing tag </strong>.

To reiterate, in HTML-speak, an **element** refers to the opening tag, the closing tag, and anything written between them. The content between the opening tag and the closing tag is referred to as **element content**. In the example above '<strong>Jung</strong>' is an element, 'Jung' is the element content, '<strong>' is the opening tag of the element, and '</strong> is the closing tag of the element.

Empty Elements

Some HTML elements do not contain any element content, meaning there is literally nothing between the opening and closing tag, neither text, nor other elements. However, these elements can still contain attributes. Examples or empty HTML elements are the <img> element, which contains information about how to display an image, and the <br> element, which simply indicates a line break.

The empty elements can be written regularly with opening and closing tags, for example as
</br>. HTML allows the option to combine both tags simply by including the closing forward slash right before the right angle bracket of the opening tag, for example <br />. In HTML5, the closing tag is no longer a requirement for empty elements and can be fully omitted.

Attributes

Attributes can extend the context and functionality of tags by allowing for the addition of extra properties to HTML elements. Attributes specify a specific value in the form:

```
attributename="attributevalue"
```

The attribute name/value pair is added right after the reserved word of the opening tag. Some attributes are used to give necessary information such as where to find an image or where a link should point to, while others simply help give the element meaning. For example, let us assume that we want our previous example, the 'Carl Jung' text, to be defined as a link:

```
<a>Carl Jung</a>
```

However, to define the actual web page to which the link would point, it is necessary to extend the functionality of the <a> tag with the href attribute. In our example, we want to link the text to the www.carljung.com web page.

```
<a href="http://www.carljung.com">Carl
Jung</a>
```

Each HTML element has a certain set of valid attributes and valid values for those attributes. A tag's properties can be expanded upon with more than one attribute. All of the attributes are included in the same opening tag of the element and are separated with an empty space. For example, the following code defines both the width and the height of an image.

```
<img width="200" height="100"></img>
```

A common question concerns the difference between tags and attributes. Generally, attributes are used when you need to describe the data itself. In other words, if it's data that's meant to be seen by the end user, it's best to mark it up in an element. If it's data that describes some other data in the document, it's best to use an attribute.

The Concept of Document Structure

Before we dive into the intricacies of the web markup language, HTML, let's look at the general concept of marking up the structure of text.

For the purpose of explaining this concept, we will create our own tags instead of using a predefined HTML set, as it will be easier to follow and understand the underlying ideas.

Let us consider the following text:

```
The Fellowship of the Ring
```

> **NOTE**
>
> End tags never contain any attributes.

We may either identify this text as the title of a book written by JRR Tolkien or as the title of a movie directed by Peter Jackson. Others might not be familiar with this text, and therefore it is necessary to mark it properly. For starters, let us consider that this text refers to a book and use a label that will identify this text as a title.

```
<title>The Fellowship of the Ring</title>
```

After that, let us add information about the author so the readers know which author wrote this book.

```
<title>The Fellowship of the Ring</title>
<author>J.R.R. Tolkien</author>
```

We can then continue to add more information about this book. For example, we can add the genre and the publication date as follows:

```
<title>The Fellowship of the Ring</title>
<author>J.R.R. Tolkien</author>
<genre>Fantasy</genre>
<published>July 29th, 1954</published>
```

Let us take this one step further and encode information about more books in the same document. The Lord of the Rings is actually a trilogy of books written by JRR Tolkien, so let us record all of them. To achieve this and separate one book from the other, we need to group the elements referring to a single book together to clearly note where one book ends and another begins. To group the elements, we will do what is known as nesting, meaning we will place one element or many elements inside another to create a meaningful group.

```
<book>
    <title>The Fellowship of the Ring</title>
    <author>J.R.R. Tolkien</author>
    <genre>Fantasy</genre>
    <published>July 29th, 1954</published>
</book>
```

With this we have defined one <book> element. As this element encloses four other elements, we can call the <book> element a parent element, and <title>, <author>, <genre> and <published>, child elements. We can now extend this document to include all books from the trilogy by simply duplicating the markup tags and changing the content within.

```
<book>
        <title> The Fellowship of the Ring</title>
        <author>J.R.R. Tolkien</author>
        <genre>Fantasy</genre>
        <published>July 29th, 1954</published>  </book>
<book>
        <title>The Two Towers</title>
        <author>J.R.R. Tolkien</author>
        <genre>Fantasy</genre>
        <published>November 11th, 1954</published>  </book>
<book>
        <title>The Return of the King</title>
        <author>J.R.R. Tolkien</author>
        <genre>Fantasy</genre>
        <published>October 20th, 1955</published>
</book>
```

The indentation of the child elements and the placement of the opening and closing tags of the parent element into separate lines are strictly for readability. For software programs that can interpret this markup, placing everything in one line would have the exact same meaning. Additionally, markup-reading applications will typically ignore all whitespace between the tags, like empty spaces, indentations or line breaks. The application simply interprets any number of consecutive spaces or tabs as a single space.

```
<book><title>The Lord of the Rings:
The Fellowship of the Ring</
 title><author>J.R.R.
Tolkien</author><genre>Fantasy</
genre><published>July 29th, 1954</
published></book>
```

However, writing markup in this manner is not conducive to reading and managing the text, therefore it is recommended to place each element on a new line.

A Little Background

HTML was originally designed as a markup language to describe the structure and semantics of a web document. The elements and attributes of HTML were supposed to indicate things such as the title of a document, what part of the text was a heading, what part of the text was a paragraph, what data belonged in a table, and so on. In its earliest form, the web was intended to transmit scientific documents so that the research community had quick and easy access to published work.

At the time, many people saw the potential of the growing web. These users started creating web pages for all different kinds of purposes, from personal home pages to huge corporate sites advertising a company's products and services. It wasn't long before web page authors wanted to control how their sites looked, and they expected the same level of control over their pages' appearance as print designers had over their creations. The web designers wanted to be able to control the fonts and colors used in documents and where their text would appear on a page. These needs and wants gave rise to what

> **NOTE**
>
> There is a higher order markup language that allows us to create our own tags, just like in this example. This language is called *Extensible Markup Language* (XML).

> **NOTE**
>
> There was never any such thing as HTML 1. The first official HTML specification was HTML 2.0.

is known as presentational or stylistic markup, because it affects the way that pages look. Stylistic markup does not describe the structure and semantics of the document, which was the initial intention of HTML. Many of the features in these specifications were driven by existing implementations of market-leading browsers as a response to user demand.

The Rise & Fall of XHTML

To keep this story short, the HTML language evolved from version 2.0 to 4.01, at which point the original purpose of structuring the document was completely lost. The people in charge of developing web standards, the World Wide Web Consortium (W3C), decided to remove all stylistic markup from HTML and rewrite it completely by using XML syntax. This new major revision was called XHTML 1.0.

The content of the XHTML 1.0 specification was identical to that of HTML 4.01; no new elements or attributes were added. As a matter of fact all presentational tags and attributes were removed, so XHTML 1.0 had fewer tags and attributes than its previous iteration.

The only major difference between XHTML 1.0 and HTML 4.01 was in the syntax of the language. While HTML allowed authors complete freedom in how they structured their elements, XHTML required authors to follow the stricter rules of XML, encouraging authors to use a single writing style. During this time period, web designers embraced the emergence of web standards, so the stricter syntax of XHTML was viewed as a "best practice" for writing markup.

Then the W3C tried to push XHTML toward an XML-based future. They published XHTML 1.1 and moved toward XHTML 2, which would be a new, pure language that was backwards compatible with neither existing web content nor previous versions of HTML. The W3C were starting to formulate theoretically pure standards unrelated to the needs of web designers and vendors who wanted emphasis placed on the creation of web applications. This caused a schism in the W3C itself, and the dissatisfied people formed their own group, the Web Hypertext Application Technology Working Group (WHATWG).

From here the story becomes so convoluted and technical that we will just skip to the part in which XHTML 2 never comes to fruition and instead the HTML5 specification becomes the new official revision of the HTML language.

HTML5

Keen to avoid the mistakes of the past, HTML5 was drafted on a series of design principles to guide its development. First, HTML5 needed to be flexible enough to support existing content, even if most of the existing content is completely messy. Second, the specification needed to be powerful enough to support the creation of web applications. Straying too far in either direction would cause it to suffer the fates of its previous brethren, HTML 4.01 and XHTML 2.

> **NOTE**
>
> The publication of XHTML 1.0 coincided with the rise of browser support for CSS; therefore it was very easy to completely move all stylistic markup away from the structure of the document.

HTML5 is now the latest version of Hypertext Markup Language, the code that describes web pages. It has been designed to deliver almost everything we would want to do online without requiring additional software such as browser plugins. HTML5 does everything from animation to movies and can be used to build incredibly complicated applications that will run in our browsers. Moreover, the web applications can still work when we are offline, and they can tell websites where we are physically located. This revision is also cross-platform, which means it works flawlessly on all systems and devices from smartphones to TV's as long as the browser supports HTML5.

Explaining the features and capabilities of HTML5 can fill a few books by itself. In the following chapters, we will first take a look at the more common HTML elements that have more or less remained the same during all revisions. Then we will focus on some of the more recent elements and functionalities exclusive to HTML5.

| 2 |
Basic Page Structure

Instead of adding to HTML's complexity, HTML5 strives to make things more intuitive. Therefore, while there is a definite learning curve with the more advanced concepts, HTML5 is much easier to learn and understand.

HTML documents are essentially simple text files that can be built with any text-editing application. You don't need any special software to create webpages. To begin it is sufficient to use the most basic text editing software you can find. On a Windows machine, this application could be Notepad.

1. In Windows, click on Start and choose All Programs > Accessories > Notepad, to open the plain Notepad text editor.
2. In Notepad's main menu, click on File and choose Save.
3. Select a destination on your computer where you will save your first web page. By default, you can select the My Documents folder.
4. In the Save As dialog window, type in sampleCV.html as a File Name and choose All Files from the Save As Type menu in order to save the document as a web page and not a .txt file.
5. Once all parameters are set, click on the Save button.

Basic Document Template

Regardless of its content, every web page has the same basic foundation for a document structure.

The <HTML> element

In an HTML document everything begins and ends with the <html> tag. This tag tells the ***browser*** that what is being read is an HTML document and should therefore be processed as a web page. The <html> tag is also known as the root of the HTML document, meaning that every other tag in the document will be placed inside this root element. To begin our web page, we will type in <html></html>, leaving a few rows in between for the other tags.

```
<html>
</html>
```

In the new HTML5 specification, the <html> tag can be extended with the manifest attribute. This attribute accepts the location of a manifest file, which in turn contains information on the document's cache. This means that the browser is instructed to store the files listed in the manifest locally on the user's computer in order to allow the user to access the page without an Internet connection. The manifest file listed in the attribute is a simple text file that lists the resources that the browser should cache for offline access. Except for offline browsing, cached resources help the page load faster and decrease the request load on the server.

Head & Body

Web pages are divided into two sections, the head and the body, with each section defined with the <head> and <body> tags respectively.

The <head> tag contains information that describes the HTML document. The information placed inside this tag is not displayed in the web browser window, but is instead used to define specific functionalities that apply to the web page. It can contain a large amount of information such as document title, scripts, styles, and meta information. This element can be used only once in

> **NOTE**
>
> When writing tags it is common practice to write the opening and the closing tags at the same time and then place the content in between. As there will be many tags written throughout web page documents, this makes it easier to ensure that all opened tags have been closed.

a web page. It starts immediately after the opening <html> tag and ends directly before the <body> tag. It contains no specific attributes that are supported in HTML5.

The body of our HTML document encloses the content of our web page. This is the part that visitors will see, including all the content such as text, links, lists tables, and images. It contains no specific attributes that are supported in HTML5. We will focus more on the body element and its subsequent content in the following chapter.

To create the head and body sections:
1. Directly after the opening HTML tag type <head>
2. Leave a few spaces for the contents of the head section
3. Type </head>
4. After the second </head> tag, type <body>
5. Leave a few spaces for the contents of the web page
6. Type </body>

At this point your document should look like this:

```
<html>
<head>

</head>
<body>

</body>
</html>
```

Additional Head Tags

One of the most important elements that is used in the head section of an HTML document is the <title> element. It is used to give your document a title, and this title is visible in the title bar of the web browser window or the browser tab of the viewed page. Additionally, the document title is the default name associated with the page when a user bookmarks the page via a browser or a third-party app. Finally, the title is also commonly used as the headline in search results from search engines like Google, directly affecting web page rankings.

The <title> element is required in every HTML document, cannot be used more than once, and cannot contain any additional tags or formatting rules.

Another popular HTML element in the head section of a web page is the <meta> element. The <meta> element is used to provide information about the document itself, such as page description, keywords, document author and other **metadata**, through the use of attributes with name/value pairs. This information is not displayed on the page but is accessible to other applications like browsers, search engine robots or other web services. .

The most common attribute in a <meta> tag is the charset attribute. This attribute specifies the character encoding for the HTML document, and the most common value is the utf-8 value. This meta information informs the browser that the content inside is encoded using the Unicode (UTF-8) character set. In turn, this allows the web browser to use the widest range of character glyphs available, so if the webpage is written in a language that uses a different script such as Arabic, or Cyrillic for Russian, the actual letters will be available and displayed on the screen.

Additionally, the <head> section can contain links to stylesheets and JavaScript files through the <link> tag, or they can be embedded into the document with the <style> tag. Stylesheets provide information on how the web page should be visually displayed, while scripts provide different kinds of interactivity and advanced functionalities. Both stylesheets and scripts are beyond the scope of this book.

1. Place the cursor between the opening and closing head tags.
2. Type <meta charset="utf-8" />
3. Type <title>.
4. Enter the title of our web page (ex. Curriculum Vitae).
5. Type </title>.

At this point our HTML document should contain the following code.

```
<html>
<head>
    <meta charset="utf-8" />
    <title>Curriculum Vitae</title>
</head>
<body>

</body>
</html>
```

We now have enough information to display this document in a web browser. The browser window will still be empty, as we have not entered any web content, but the title bar will display the name that we placed inside the <title> element **(Figure 1)**.

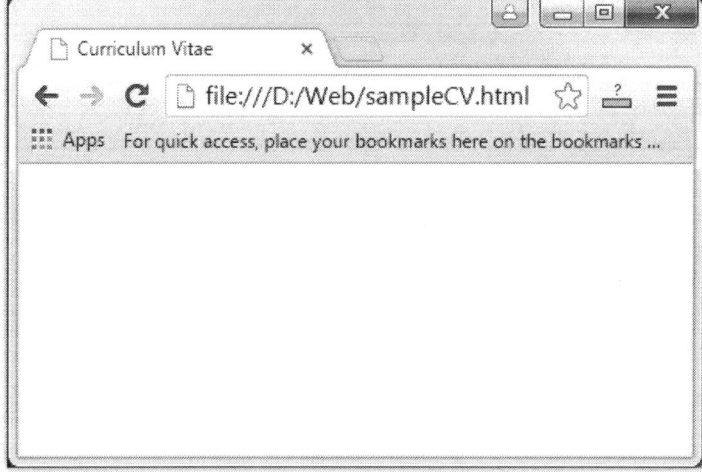

Fg. 1 : Displaying the document title.

Document Declaration

With so many HTML specifications, how is the web browser supposed to know to correctly parse the document? The absolute top of any HTML document contains one additional element called a **DOCTYPE** declaration. The DOCTYPE declaration is an instruction found above the opening <html> tag that tells the web browser what version of HTML the document uses. For HTML5 we simply write the following piece of code:

```
<!doctype html>
<html>
<head>
```

The DOCTYPE declaration isn't exactly a tag or an *element*. As its name states, it is simply a declaration. HTML5 has greatly simplified the DOCTYPE declaration, as in previous revisions this was a very illegible piece of code. The following example is the DOCTYPE declaration for the HTML 4.01 Strict specification.

```
<!DOCTYPE html PUBLIC "-//W3C//DTD HTML 4.01 Strict//EN" "http://www.w3.org/TR/html4/strict.dtd">
```

If for any reason we don't want to use the HTML5 DOCTYPE, our second choice should be the HTML 4.01 Strict DOCTYPE. The "strict" part refers to the removal of all the *deprecated* tags, and it is great for pages that are absolutely correct against the standard. With that said, our main document structure for the sample CV should look like this:

```
<!DOCTYPE html>
<html>
<head>
    <meta charset="utf-8" />
    <title>Curriculum Vitae</title>
</head>
<body>
</body>
</html>
```

| 3 |
Page Content

As mentioned previously, all the visible content is placed within the <body> tag. Since HTML is all about proper document markup, initially we have to view the text in the document as headings, paragraphs and lists.

Paragraphs & Line Breaks

To define a paragraph of text we will use the <p> element. Paragraphs are the first and the most common levels of structure for web page text. To define a paragraph, we simply enclose the text in between the opening and the closing <p> tag.

```
<p>Name: Scott Johnson</p>
```

When we put several paragraphs in a row, the browser separates the paragraphs by approximately a half line of text by default. However, if the paragraph is empty, the browser will completely ignore the element, and it won't display it as an extra line break **(Figure 2)**.

```
<p>Name: Scott Johnson</p>
<p>Occupation: Web Designer</p>
<p></p>
<p>Date of birth: 09/09/1980</p>
```

Sometimes we will have to start a new line of text without using the paragraph element. For example, we want to include our address in our CV, and we want it in the standard single-spaced three-line format. In situations like this, we will use the standalone line break element <br>.

The <br> element tells a browser to move the text to the start of the following line (Figure 3).

```
<p>Address:<br>
523 Beaumont Way<br>
Santa Rosa<br>
California 52409</p>
```

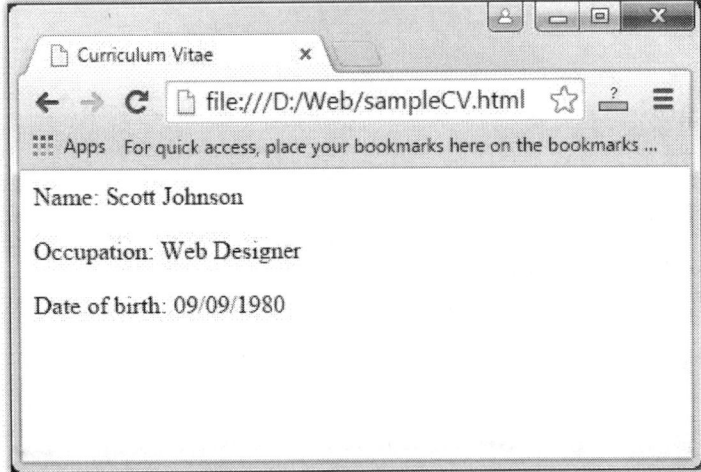

Fg. 2: Visual representation of paragraphs.

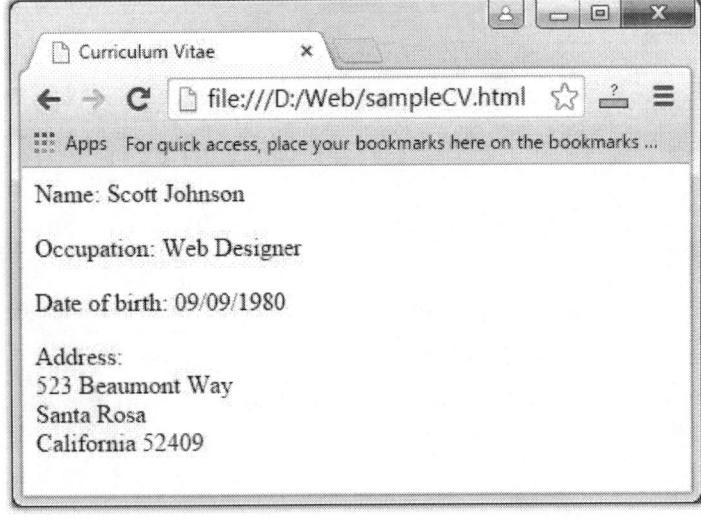

Fg. 3: Visual representation of line breaks.

We have to be careful not the misuse line breaks. We don't need to perfect our paragraphs, as the browser will rewrap the text differently in different resolutions and browser sizes. Additionally, we shouldn't be concerned about the amount of space between regular paragraphs; this concerns appearance and is manageable via CSS. A good rule for using line breaks is to avoid them in regular paragraphs and use them to force breaks in addresses, outlines, poems, and other types of text that structurally require tighter flow control.

what about empty spaces?

We have already learned that browsers ignore extra spaces and line breaks in the HTML, so what happens in the rare situation in which we need to use additional spaces? Well, in HTML empty space is treated like a special character and needs to be entered as a special code, . The & symbol signals to the browser that a code for a special character will follow; the nbsp is the code for the special character, which in this case is a short-hand for non-breaking space, while the semicolon (;) signals to the browser that the code for the special character has ended and from here on out the text should be treated as normal.

Creating Headings

Headings are typically used as section titles above paragraphs. They help define the hierarchy of our document with larger headings identifying more important topics and smaller headings denoting issues of lesser importance within the context of that larger topic. To make sure our document follows a logical outline, we will always start with the largest heading (level 1) and work our way down.

HTML supports up to six levels of headings starting at <h1>, the largest, and finishing with <h6>, the smallest, although headings below <h4> are seldom necessary. This helps separate the document into a proper and more readable structure. By default, the browser will display headings in boldface at various sizes, depending on the heading level **(Figure 4)**.

To organize our web page with headers:

1. In the body section of our HTML document, type <hn>, in which n is a number from 1 to 6, depending on the level of header that we want to create.
2. Type the contents of the header.
3. Type </hn> in which n is the same number used in step 1.

By including headings, the content for our CV web page would look like this:

```
<!DOCTYPE html>
<html>
<head>
    <meta charset="utf-8">
    <title>Curriculum Vitae</title>
</head>
<body>
<h1>Curriculum Vitae</h1>
<h2>Personal Info</h2>
<p>Name: Scott Johnson</p>
<p>Occupation: Web Designer</p>
<p>Date of birth: 09/09/1980</p>
<p>Address: <br>
523 Beaumont Way<br>
Santa Rosa<br>
California 52409</p>

<h2>Education</h2>

<h2>Skills</h2>
</body>
</html>
```

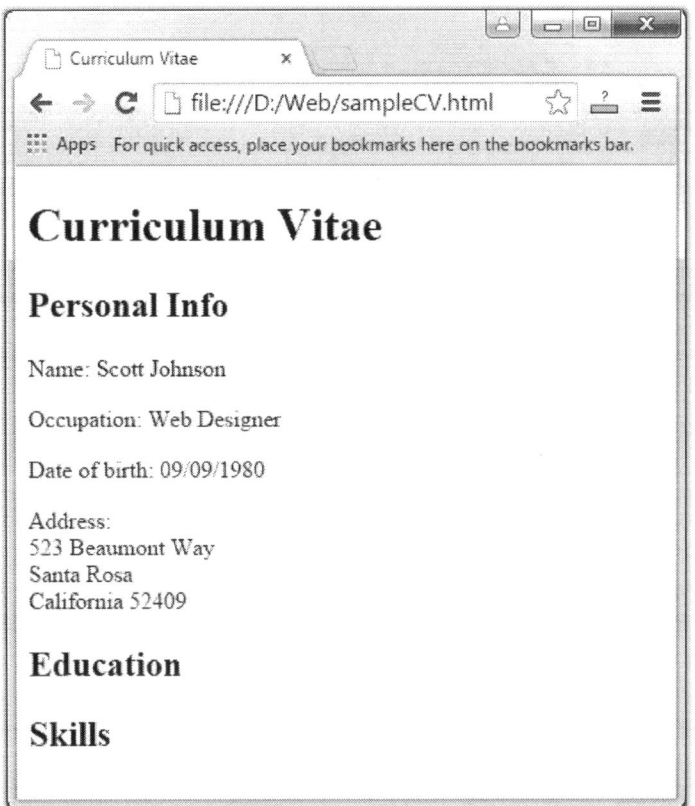

> **NOTE**
>
> The actual look of headings can be controlled with stylesheets.

Fg. 4 : CV with headings and paragraphs

Lists

HTML allows three different kinds of lists. Two of the list types, ordered and unordered, are commonly used in everyday writing, while the third type, definition list, is not so common.

- Ordered lists are meant to present items in a sequential order when the order of the items is important. A sequential number or letter precedes each item.
- Unordered lists, commonly referred to as a bullet point lists, are the most frequently used lists on the web. They itemize things without implying a sequence, so a bullet precedes each item.
- Description lists display terms that need to be followed by a definition or a description. As they are meant to hold glossary items (ex. a dictionary), and no symbols are needed to precede them.

Ordered Lists

The ordered list is perfect for explaining step-by-step instructions to complete a particular task. To create an ordered list, we use the <ol> element. As this element defines the list as a whole, every subsequent item on the list has to be defined with the <li> element, with all <li> elements contained within the <ol> element.

The following example presents a list of top 5 movies of all time **(Figure 5)**.

```
<ol>
    <li>Avatar</li>
    <li>Titanic</li>
    <li>The Avengers</li>
    <li>Harry Potter</li>
    <li>Frozen</li>
</ol>
```

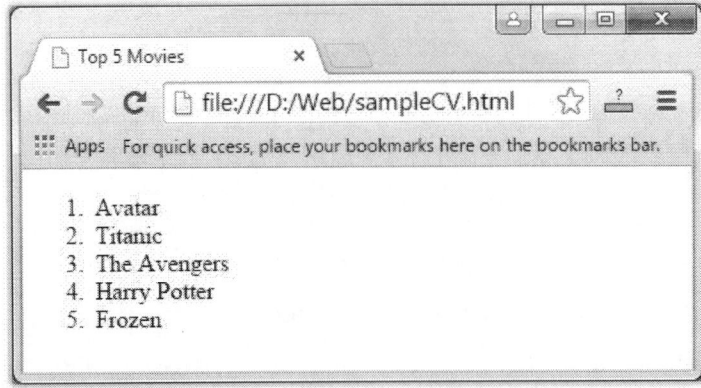

Fg. 5 : List of top 5 movies.

In an ordered list, HTML will consecutively number each item starting with the value '1' unless otherwise specified. We will not need to supply the numbers; instead, the browser will automatically add the appropriate number in front of each list item. This allows us to insert and remove list items without messing up the numbering scheme. By default, the browser will align and indent the list items and insert some space between the paragraph preceding the list and the list itself.

Ordered lists can be extended with three attributes: start, type and reversed.

- The **start** attribute lets us start the list at a value other than 1. However, there is no way to continue the numbering from a previous list.
- The **type** attribute lets us choose the numbering styles from numbers, roman numerals and letters. The values for type attribute are presented in **Table 1**.
- The **reversed** attribute, which is exclusive to HTML5, allows us to specify the list numbering in a descending order. This attribute doesn't come with any values.

ATTRIBUTE VALUE	NUMBERING	EXAMPLE
1	Numbers	1,2,3
a	Lowercase Letters	a,b,c
A	Uppercase Letters	A,B,C
i	Lowercase Roman Numerals	i,ii,iii
I	Uppercase Roman Numerals	I,II,III

Table 1 : Types of ordered lists.

The following example will reverse the numbering in the list of top 5 movies **(Figure 6)**:

```
<ol reversed>
    <li>Frozen</li>
    <li>Harry Potter</li>
    <li>The Avengers</li>
    <li>Titanic</li>
    <li>Avatar</li>
</ol>
```

HTML QUICKSTART GUIDE

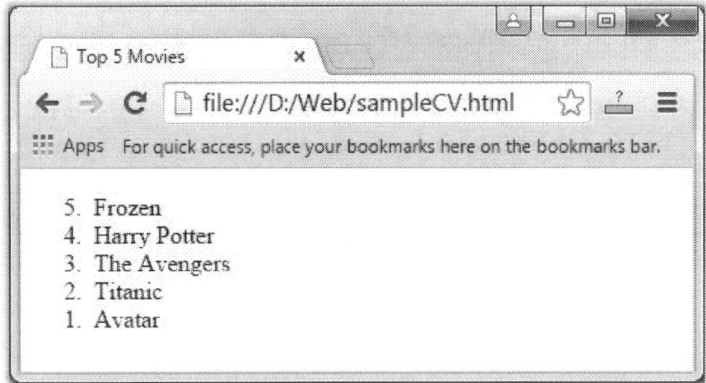

Fg. 6 : Descending list of top 5 movies.

Unordered Lists

Unordered lists are very similar to ordered lists but with bullets rather than numbers to precede the list items. They are the most widely used lists on the web for a series of items that requires no particular order. For unordered lists, we use the <ul> element as a substitute for the <ol> element, but each item on the list will remain defined by the <li> element.

As an example let's use an unordered list to present the Education section in our sample CV **(Figure 7)**:

```
<ul>
    <li>PhD in Computer Science at MIT</li>
    <li>Bachelor of Computer Science at MIT</li>
    <li>Santa Rosa High School</li>
</ul>
```

The unordered list has no attributes that are supported by HTML5.

> **NOTE**
> For both ordered and unordered lists, no text is permitted between the opening list tag (ol or ul) and the first li tag.

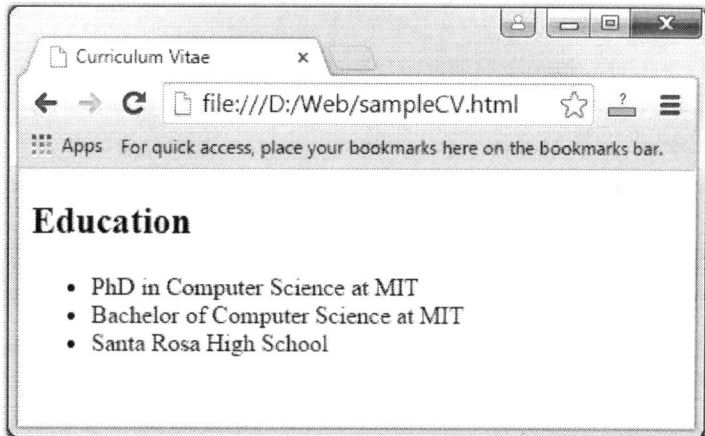

Fg. 7: Unordered list for Education section.

Nesting Lists

While lists work well on their own, we may create lists within a list, also known as nesting lists. This technique allows us to build multilayered outlines and detailed sequences of instructions. We can even mix ordered and unordered lists.

To nest a list, we declare a new list, <ol> or <ul>, inside a <li> element of an existing list. For example **(Figure 8)**, we can reorganize our Education list in our sample CV as follows:

```
<ul>
    <li>MIT</li>
    <ul>
        <li>PhD Degree in Computer Science</li>
        <li>Bachelor Degree in Computer Science</li>
    </ul>
    <li>Santa Rosa High School</li>
</ul>
```

HTML QUICKSTART GUIDE

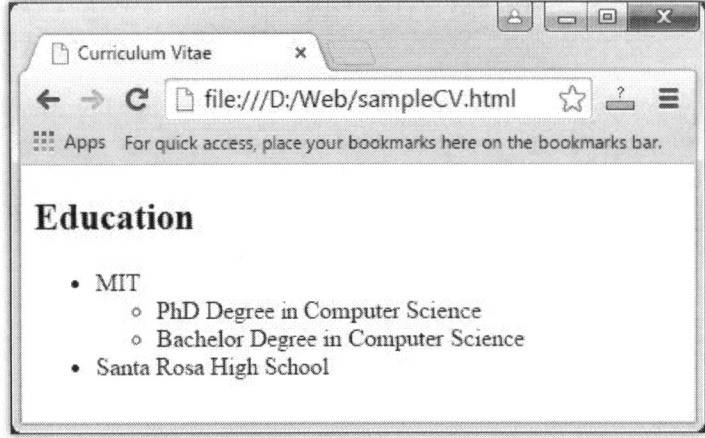

Fg. 8 : Nested list for Education section.

Description Lists

HTML provides a third type of list called a description list. In previous HTML revisions, the name "definition list" was used instead of "description list." This type of list has a slightly different structure than unordered and ordered lists and is well suited for glossaries and dictionaries. It can work well with any text structure that needs to pair a word or a phrase with a longer description.

The description list is defined by the <dl> element. Each description list item contains two parts: a term and a description. The term is used to define a term/name and utilizes the <dt> element. The definition element, <dd>, follows the <dt> element and is used to describe the term/name.

In the HTML5 specification, no additional attributes are supported for any description list element.

NOTE

When using description lists, it is possible to define multiple descriptions for one item by adding each description in an additional <dd> element.

32

The following description list example defines the different ways to prepare espresso **(Figure 9)**:

```
<dl>
<dt>Cappucinno</dt>
<dd>1 part espresso, 1 part hot milk, steamed milk foam</dd>
<dt>Macchiato</dt>
<dd>1 part espresso, 1 part foamed milk, shaved cocoa</dd>
<dt>Espresso</dt>
<dd>1 part espresso, 0 parts of anything else</dd>
</dl>
```

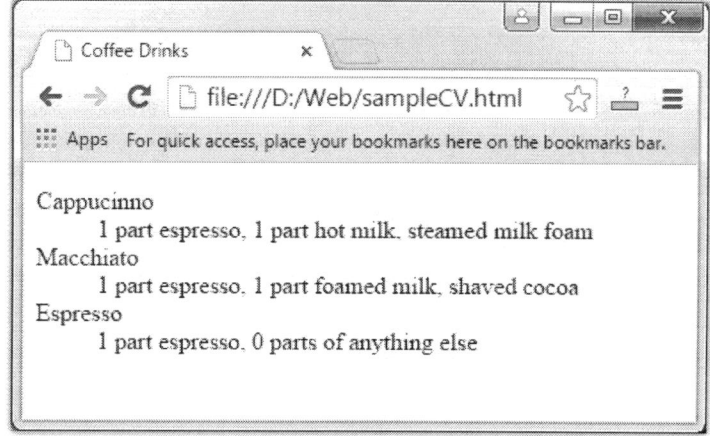

Fg. 9: Definition list for different espresso drinks.

Quotations

We can indicate that a selection of text is quoted from another source using the <blockquote> element. The <blockquote> element only indicatesthat its content was sourced from somewhere else, so we still need to use elements such as headlines and paragraphs to mark up the quotation's content. For shorter quotations that don't need additional document structure, we can use the <q> element. Both the <blockquote> and the <q> elements can be extended with the cite attribute. The cite attribute specifies the URL source of the quotation.

An example for <blockquote> is:

```
<blockquote cite="http://www.worldwildlife.org/who/index.html">
<p> For 50 years, WWF has been protecting the future of nature. The world's leading conservation organization, WWF works in 100 countries and is supported by 1.2 million members in the United States and close to 5 million globally.</p>
</blockquote>
```

A short quote, <q> example is:

```
<p>WWF's goal is to: <q cite="http://www.wwf.org">Build a future where people live in harmony with nature.</q>We hope they succeed.</p>
```

Additional Text Elements

The HTML5 specification contains additional tags that give text different semantic meanings. These tags have either been inherited and redefined from previous HTML revisions or are brand new for this latest iteration. Here are some of the more commonly used tags:

- **<em>** is used to stress emphasis. The emphasis is linguistic; if spoken it would emphasize pronunciation on a word, which would change the nuance of the sentence. By default the browser renders the <em> element as italic text.
- **<strong>** is used to show strong importance for its content as defined by the user. By default the browser renders the <strong> element as bold text.
- **<small>** is used for side comments such as small print, a copyright statement, a disclaimer and similar items.
- **<mark>** is a new HTML5 element used to indicate text that we are specifically trying to highlight without changing its importance or emphasis. The mark element represents a run of text in one document marked or highlighted for reference purposes due to its relevance in another context.

- **<sub>** defines subscript text. Subscript text is mostly used in math and chemistry formulas. It will appear bellow the normal line and will often be rendered in a smaller font.
- **<sup>** defines superscript text. Superscript text is mostly used in footnotes or math. It will appear half a character above the normal line and will often be rendered in a smaller font.
- **<abbr>** defines an abbreviation. This element is usually extended with the title attribute to show the full version of the abbreviation/acronym when we mouse the cursor over the marked content.
- **<hr>** is a horizontal rule used for a paragraph-level thematic break, which indicates a change in topic. By default the browser presents the <hr> element as a horizontal line.

In our CV example **(Figure 10)** we can use the <strong> element to indicate the importance of the text labels within the Personal Info section.

```
<h2>Personal Info</h2>
<p><strong>Name:</strong> Scott Johnson</p>
<p><strong>Occupation:</strong> Web Designer</p>
<p><strong>Date of birth:</strong> 09/09/1980</p>
<p><strong>Address:</strong><br>
523 Beaumont Way<br>
Santa Rosa<br>
California 52409</p>
```

HTML QUICKSTART GUIDE

Fg. 10 : Important elements for the Personal Info section.

We can also use the <sup> and <sub> elements to note names of specific companies in our Portfolio **(Figure 11)**.

```
<h2>Portfolio</h2>
<p>I have worked as a freelance web designer for the following companies:</p>
<ul>
  <li>H<sub>2</sub>O Wireless - a broadband Internet provider</li>
  <li>DSQUARED<sup>2</sup> - an international fashion house</li>
</ul>
```

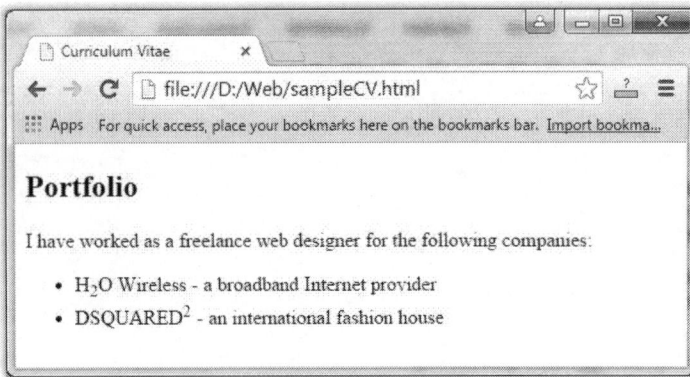

Fg. 11 : Superscript and subscript elements for the Portfolio section.

We can use the <abbr> element to define the acronyms in the Skills section, both HTML and CSS **(Figure 12)**.

```
<h2>Skills</h2>
<p>I have expert coding knowledge in the core web technologies: <abbr title="HyperText Markup Language">HTML</abbr>, <abbr title="Cascading StyleSheets">CSS</abbr> and JavaScript.</p>
```

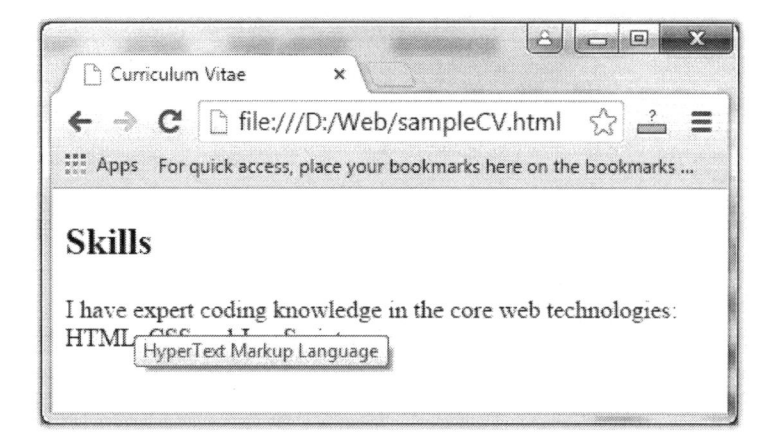

Fg. 12 : Abbreviation for the Skills section.

And we can separate our sections with an <hr> element.

After these examples, our sample CV will approximately have the following structure **(Figure 13)**:

```
<!DOCTYPE html>
<html>
<head>
    <meta charset="utf-8">
    <title>Curriculum Vitae</title>
</head>
<body>
<h1>Curriculum Vitae</h1>
<h2>Personal Info</h2>
```

HTML QUICKSTART GUIDE

```
<p><strong>Name:</strong> Scott Johnson</p>
<p><strong>Occupation:</strong> Web Designer</p>
<p><strong>Date of birth:</strong> 09/09/1980</p>
<p><strong>Address:</strong><br>
523 Beaumont Way<br>
Santa Rosa<br>
California 52409</p><hr>
<h2>Education</h2>
<ul>
    <li>MIT</li>
      <ul>
          <li>PhD Degree in Computer Science</li>
          <li>Bachelor Degree in Computer Science</li>
      </ul>
    <li>Santa Rosa High School</li>
</ul>
<hr>
<h2>Skills</h2>
<p>I have expert coding knowledge in the core web technologies: <abbr title="HyperText Markup Language">HTML</abbr>, <abbr title="Cascading StyleSheets">CSS</abbr> and JavaScript.</p>
<hr>
<h2>Portfolio</h2>
<p>I have worked as a freelance web designer for the following companies:</p>
<ul>
    <li>H<sub>2</sub>O Wireless - a broadband Internet provider</li>
    <li>DSQUARED<sup>2</sup> - an international fashion house</li>
</ul>
</body>
</html>
```

Curriculum Vitae

Personal Info

Name: Scott Johnson

Occupation: Web Designer

Date of birth: 09/09/1980

Address:
523 Beaumont Way
Santa Rosa
California 52409

Education

- MIT
    - PhD Degree in Computer Science
    - Bachelor Degree in Computer Science
- Santa Rosa High School

Skills

I have expert coding knowledge in the core web technologies: HTML, CSS and JavaScript.

Portfolio

I have worked as a freelance web designer for the following companies:

- H_2O Wireless - a broadband Internet provider
- DSQUARED^2 - an international fashion house

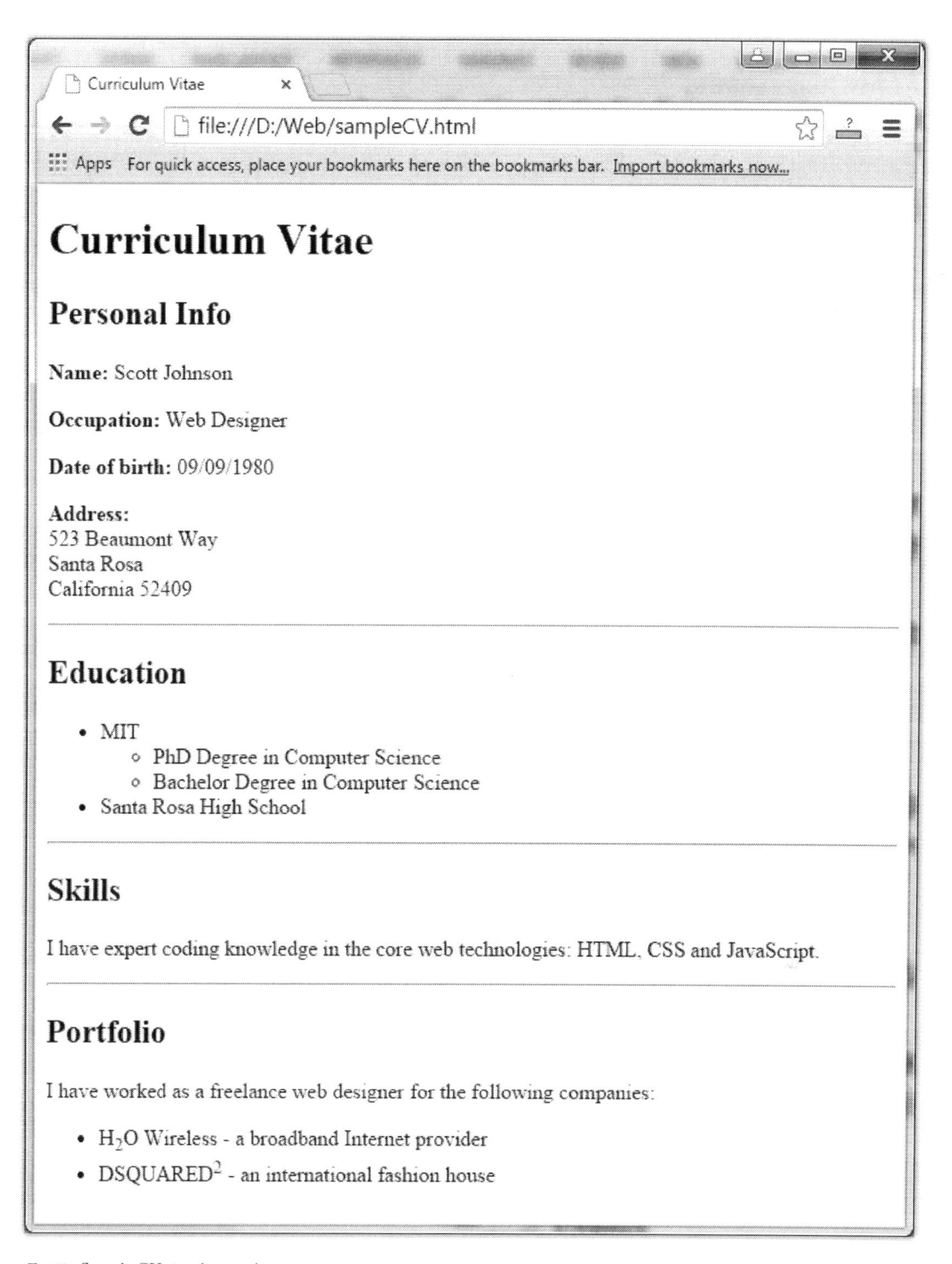

Fg. 13: Sample CV visual example.

Tables

When we want to mark up data that would be best presented in a table, we need to create HTML tables. Tabular data usually reminds us of spreadsheets, but HTML tables are slightly different from spreadsheets tables because they consist of rows and cells in a row. There is no need to define a number of columns, as the number of cells in each row determines how many columns a table will have. Nevertheless, marking up tabular data is relatively easy, as HTML provides us with plenty of semantic elements for data organization.

The starting point for every HTML table is the <table> element. Let us start adding a table to redesign the Skills section in our sample CV.

```
<table>
</table>
```

Using just a <table> tag is not sufficient to create the table; we need to add a table row with the <tr> element.

```
<table>
<tr>
</tr>
</table>
```

Finally, we need to add a few cells in this row in order to have a basic table displayed in our browser. When discussing HTML table semantics, we must be aware that there are two type of elements to represent table cells: <td> and <th>. The <td> element stands for table data and represents a regular cell that contains data. The <th> element stands for table header and defines a cell that contains a heading for a table row or a column.

In our example, in the first row we will insert two header cells one for 'Web Technology' and the other for 'Skill Level'.

```
<table>
<tr>
        <th>Web Technology</th>
        <th>Skill Level</th>
</tr>
</table>
```

To complete our table, we will insert three more rows. In these rows, instead of <th> we will use the <td> element for representing cells, as these cells will contain actual data and no headings (**Figure 14**). Our final table code will look like this:

```
<table>
<tr>
        <th>Web Technology</th>
        <th>Skill Level</th>
</tr>
<tr>
        <td>HTML</td>
        <td>Expert</td>
</tr>
<tr>
        <td>CSS</td>
        <td>Expert</td>
</tr>
<tr>
        <td>JavaScript</td>
        <td>Advanced</td>
</tr>
</table>
```

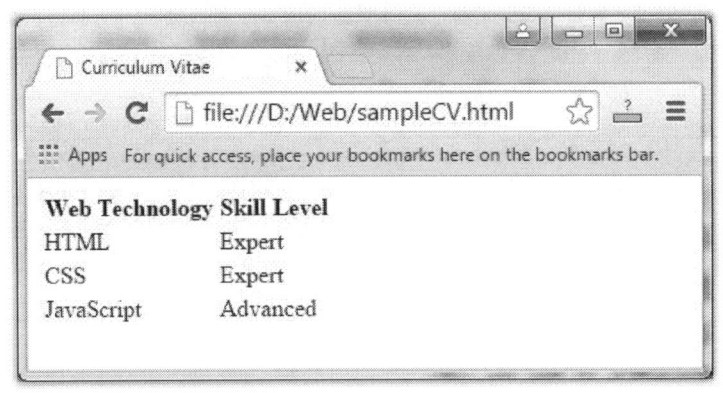

Fg. 14 : Table representation.

This basic table doesn't have any borders, but the data appears in neatly lined rows and columns. Borders and additional visual table properties are managed through CSS.

The final structure of our sample CV is displayed on the following pages.

NOTE

Tables have a long web history. While originally conceived just to hold tabular data, they were quickly misused for a much bigger task: serving as the foundation for complicated page layouts with features that were impossible before the advent of CSS.

```html
<!DOCTYPE html>
    <html>
    <head>
        <meta charset="utf-8">
        <title>Curriculum Vitae</title>
    </head>
    <body>
    <h1>Curriculum Vitae</h1>
    <h2>Personal Info</h2>
    <p><strong>Name:</strong> Scott Johnson</p>
    <p><strong>Occupation:</strong> Web Designer</p>
    <p><strong>Date of birth:</strong> 09/09/1980</p>
    <p><strong>Address:</strong> <br>
    523 Beaumont Way<br>
    Santa Rosa<br>
    California 52409</p>
    <hr>
    <h2>Education</h2>
    <ul>
        <li>MIT</li>
            <ul>
                <li>PhD Degree in Computer Science</li>
                <li>Bachelor Degree in Computer Science</li>
            </ul>
        <li>Santa Rosa High School</li>
    </ul>
    <hr>
    <h2>Skills</h2>
    <table>
    <tr>
        <th>Web Technology</th>
        <th>Skill Level</th>
```

```
    </tr>
    <tr>
        <td>HTML</td>
        <td>Expert</td>
    </tr>
    <tr>
        <td>CSS</td>
        <td>Expert</td>
    </tr>
    <tr>
        <td>JavaScript</td>
        <td>Advanced</td>
    </tr>
</table>
<hr>
<h2>Portfolio</h2>
<p>I have worked as a freelance web designer for the following companies:</p>
<ul>
    <li>H<sub>2</sub>O Wireless - a broadband Internet provider</li>
    <li>DSQUARED<sup>2</sup> - an international fashion house</li>
</ul>
</body>
</html>
```

Special Characters

Not all characters available on the web are available on our keyboards. So what happens when we want to add special characters like a copyright symbol (©) or a degree (°)? HTML supports all these characters along with about 250 relatives, including mathematical symbols and special letters. To add them to our web page, we need to use what is known as an HTML character entity. An HTML character entity is initiated by the ampersand (&) symbol, followed by a keyword (or ASCII code) and concluded with the semicolon (;) symbol. For example, the HTML character code for a *non-breaking space* will be written as .

Other HTML character entities are presented in the following table:

CHARACTER	NAME OF CHARACTER	CODE
<	Left angle bracket	&lt;
>	Right angle bracket	&gt;
&	Ampersand	&amp;
"	Double quotation mark	&quot;
©	Copyright	&copy;
®	Registered trademark	&reg;
¢	Cent sign	&cent;
£	Pound sterling	&pound;
€	Euro sign	&euro;
°	Degree sign	&deg;
±	Plus or minus	&plusmn;
µ	Micro sign	&micro;
½	Fraction one-half	&frac12;

Table 2 : HTML character entities.

Inserting Images

We can place all kinds of images on our web page, from logos to photographs. Web images appear automatically when the visitor jumps to our page, as long as the browser is configured to view them.

To place an image in a web document, we use the <img> element. The image does not reside in the web page. It is stored as a separate file, and the HTML code points to its location. Technically, an image element is an empty element, as it will be replaced by the actual referenced image content. As an empty element, it consists only of attributes and is opened and closed in a single tag.

To point to the actual image that we want to display, we use the src attribute to insert the relative or absolute path to the image.

```
<img src="images\cv_picture.jpg">
```

When a browser reads this <img> element, it sends out a request for the cv_picture.jpg file from the images folder. After retrieving the file, the browser will insert that picture into the page in the location of the <img> tag.

We are also strongly encouraged to use the alt attribute along with the <img> attribute. Short for alternate text, this attribute is used to describe the image and its meaning in words in order to give it context in the document.

```
<img src="images\cv_picture.jpg"
alt="Scott Johnson profile picture">
```

> **NOTE**
>
> While alternate text can theoretically be as long as we like, most browsers don't automatically wrap long lines. Therefore, it's a good idea to keep it under 50 characters.

Usually, alternate text doesn't show up on the web page with the image, but it provides several important features. First, in keeping with the semantic importance of markup, it lets the image provide some meaning to the document. Without the alternate text in the <img> element, the image would be essentially "meaningless," and the document would lose some of its semantic value. Second, from a more functional perspective, the browser will display the alternate text if it can't display the image itself for any reason. Finally, and most importantly, the alternate text acts as an ***accessibility*** tool for visitors who are visually impaired and use a screen-reading program to access our website.

When working with web images, we have to consider two variables: image dimensions and image file size. Image dimensions determine how much screen real estate an image occupies in pixels. The image file size will determine the time it will take for that image to be transferred over the Internet from a web server to a browser client. While parsing the code, when a browser reaches the img tag, it must first load the image to see how big it is and how much space it will consume on the screen. If we specify the image's dimensions, the browser can reserve some screen space and load the rest of the page content as the image loads.

The <img> element lets us specify the image dimensions through its optional height and width attributes. If we want to use the original dimensions of the image, we need to take the following steps:

1. In Windows Explorer right-click the image.
2. Choose Properties from the contextual pop-up menu. A box will appear showing the dimensions of our image in pixels.

Once we figure out the size of our image, we can use the width and height attributes to specify the width and height of our image in pixels. The width and height attributes don't necessarily have to reflect the actual size of the image, as we can insert any value we want.

```
<img src="images\cv_picture.jpg" alt="Scott Johnson profile picture" width="100" height ="150">
```

In the above example, we tell the browser to reserve 100x150 pixels of screen estate in which to load the cv_picture.jpg image from the images folder.

> **NOTE**
>
> Some HTML editors, like Dreamweaver and Expression Web, will automatically add the height and width attributes when you insert an image.

web images

Web browsers are not capable of displaying every image type; rather, are limited only to formats that offer very high compression rates in order to provide smaller image sizes. This limits our options to only three formats: JPEG, GIF and PNG, and partially SVG.

- *JPEG* is suitable for photos that can tolerate some loss of quality. The JPEG format compresses an image's file size so that it downloads faster. It doesn't work well if the picture contains text or line art.

- *GIF* is suitable for graphics with very few colors like simple logos or clip art. It is limited to 256 colors and gives horrible results when used for compressing photographic images.

- *PNG* is a format created specifically for the web and is suitable for all kinds of images. It doesn't always compress as well as JPEG, but it is particularly good for small, sharp graphics, and it is used as a more powerful replacement for the GIF standard.

- *SVG* is an up-and-coming standard for vector drawings with a number of advantages, including small size and flexibility, as you can resize SVG images without losing detail or producing blurry images. It is not supported by Internet Explorer versions 8 and earlier, so it is not yet a viable choice for web graphics.

Links

Creating a single web page is an important step in building a website, but we need more than one page to complete the website, and these pages will need to be connected so a visitor can easily jump from one page to another via links. Furthermore, we also want to create connections to web pages on other websites.

All links, officially called hyperlinks, are managed through the so-called ***anchor*** element, <a>.

```
<a>Link to page</a>
```

The <a> element has no function by itself. To be a fully functioning link, it must have a destination to specify what happens when the visitor clicks the link. The most common links load a new page, but they can also show an image, play a sound or movie, download files, open a newsgroup, send an e-mail message, run a CGI program, and more. To define a destination, we extend the <a> element with the href attribute, which is shorthand for "hypertext reference," and define a URL. By default the browser displays text links as blue underlined text.

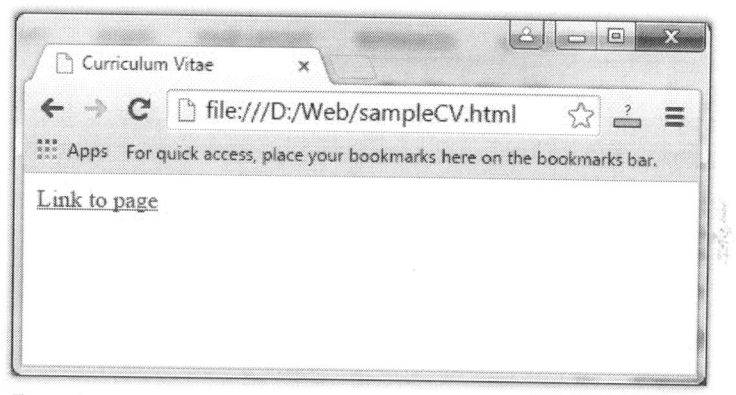

```
<a href="page.html">Link to page</a>
```

Fig. 15 : Link example.

The text between the opening and closing tags of the <a> element is also known as a label, the part the visitor sees and clicks to reach the destination. This text in itself is very important since search engines index it in a special way and pay special attention to the actual content of the link. Hence it is advisable to use descriptive text (ex. Products, Register, About) instead of vague words such as "click here," "more," or "this link."

Two additional attributes that extend the functionality of the <a> element can be very helpful when it comes to links:

- **Target** : The target attribute specifies where we want to open the linked document. The most common value we use for the target attribute is _blank, when we want the link to open in a new tab/browser window, instead of the current window (ex. <a href="sample_cv.html" target="_blank">).

- **Download** : The download attribute specifies that the target will be downloaded when a user clicks on the hyperlink instead of displayed in the web browser window (ex. <a href="thesis_document.pdf" download>Get the Thesis Document</a>).

Link Types

We are obviously not limited to creating internal links, or links to other web pages on our own website. Alternatively, we can create external links that will point to pages or resources on other websites.

To create an external link, we need to use an absolute URL, meaning we have to set the complete address of the page including the protocol. For example, the following link will point to the W3Schools page that explains the <a> element:

```
<a href="http://www.w3schools.com/tags/tag_th.asp">More information about HTML links</a>
```

A mailto link helps users send an email message. When a user clicks on a mailto link, the web browser will open the default email program and begin creating a new email message.

To create a mailto link, we need to specify a value in the href attribute that starts with the word "mailto," followed by a colon (:) and our email address. For example,

```
<a href="mailto:contact@samplecv.com">contact@samplecv.com </a>
```

Notice that we used the email address as a label for this mailto link instead of something vague like "Email Us." We did this because the mailto link doesn't always work for users that have web-based email services like Gmail. Providing the actual address will help them get the actual email contact information if they can't click on the link.

If we create a link to a file that the browser does not know how to handle (ex. a Word or Excel file), the browser will either try to open a helper program to view the file or will try to download it to the user's hard disk.

Bookmarks

Most links on our website will lead us from one page to another. When we click on a link and a new page is loaded, by default we are taken to the top of the indicated page, but the link doesn't always have to point to the top. We can also create links to specific parts of a page. This is particularly useful when we want to direct the user to a particular segment of a long, scrolling page. The position on the page to which we send the user is a specific tag called a fragment. We can create links to fragments on the current web page or to a specific fragment on another web page.

Creating a link that points to a fragment is a two-step process:

First we identify the tag to which we will point by extending the tag with the id attribute. The id attribute assigns a unique name to any HTML element. For instance, let us say that in our CV sample we want to create a navigation menu that will point to different fragments of the CV. And let us assume that we want these fragments to be defined at each <h2> heading: Personal Information, Education, Skills and Portfolio. We need to identify the headings that we want to point to and we will do this as follows:

```
<h2 id="education">Education</h2>
```

By placing an id attribute in the <h2> heading, we have effectively created a bookmark.

Second, we create a link that points to this bookmark. To do this, we add the number-sign symbol (#) followed by the bookmark name in the href attribute of an <a> element. For example:

```
<a href="#education">Education</a>
```

We can also create a link to a bookmark on a different page. All we need to do is append the bookmark to the end of the URL. For example:

```
<a href="sample_cv.html#education">
Education</a>
```

When users click on this link the browser will first take them to the sample_cv.html page and then scroll them down until they reach the #education bookmark.

Let's continue and create bookmark links to all <h2> headings in our sample CV.

The final code should look something like **Figure 16**

You can find the final sample code displayed on the following pages.

NOTE

When our bookmark is near the bottom of a page, a browser might not be able to scroll the bookmark all the way to the top of its window if there is insufficient content. Instead, the bookmarked section will appear somewhere in the middle of the browser window.

```html
<!DOCTYPE html>
<html>
<head>
    <meta charset="utf-8">
    <title>Curriculum Vitae</title>
</head>
<body>
<h1>Curriculum Vitae</h1>
<p><img  src="images\cv_picture.jpg"  alt="Scott  Johnson  profile picture" width="100" height ="150">
</p>
<p><a href="#personal">Personal Information</a></p>
<p><a href="#education">Education</a></p>
<p><a href="#skills">Skills</a></p>
<p><a href="#portfolio">Portfolio</a></p>
<h2 id="personal">Personal Info</h2>
<p><strong>Name:</strong> Scott Johnson</p>
<p><strong>Occupation:</strong> Web Designer</p>
<p><strong>Date of birth:</strong> 09/09/1980</p>
<p><strong>Address:</strong> <br>
523 Beaumont Way<br>
Santa Rosa<br>
California 52409</p>
<hr>
<h2>Education</h2>
<ul>
    <li>MIT</li>
        <ul>
            <li>PhD Degree in Computer Science</li>
            <li>Bachelor Degree in Computer Science</li>
        </ul>
    <li>Santa Rosa High School</li>
```

```html
    </ul>
    <hr>
    <h2 id="skills">Skills</h2>
    <table>
    <tr>
        <th>Web Technology</th>
        <th>Skill Level</th></tr>
    <tr>
        <td>HTML</td>
        <td>Expert</td>
    </tr>
    <tr>
        <td>CSS</td>
        <td>Expert</td></tr>
    <tr>
        <td>JavaScript</td>
        <td>Advanced</td>
    </tr>
    </table>
    <hr>
    <h2 id="portfolio">Portfolio</h2>
    <p>I have worked as a freelance web designer for the following companies:</p>
    <ul>
        <li>H<sub>2</sub>O Wireless - a broadband Internet provider</li>
        <li>DSQUARED<sup>2</sup> - an international fashion house</li>
    </ul>
    </body>
    </html>
```

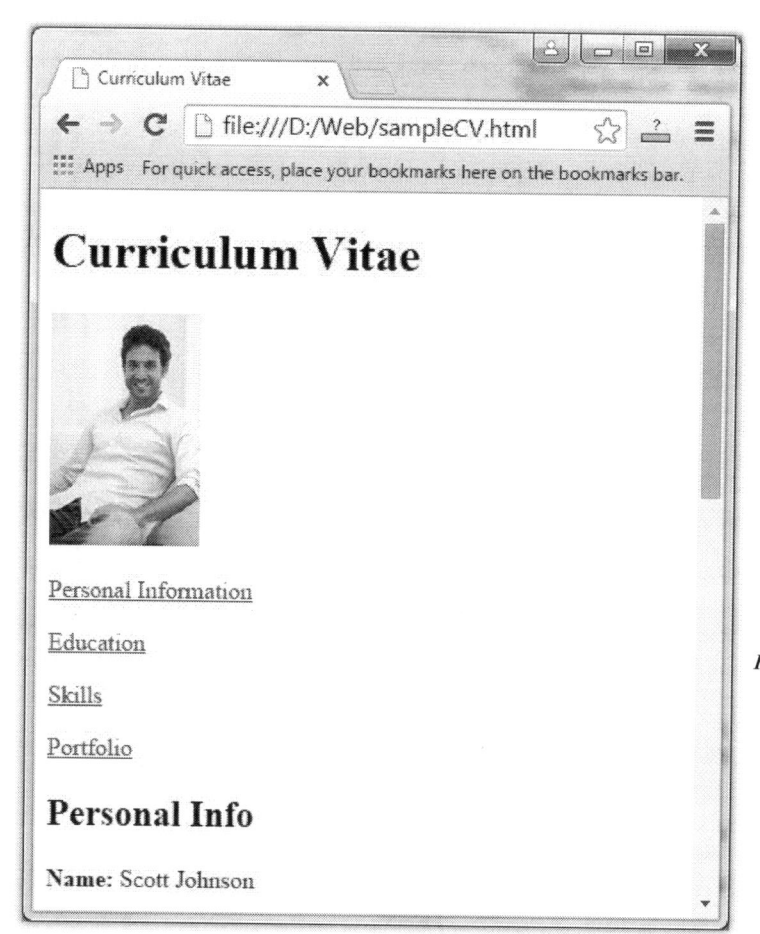

Fg. 16 : Partial view of sample CV.

HTML Comments

A *comment* is a piece of code that is fully ignored by any web browser. The reason for its existence is to either provide information about the code or to remove sections of the code but leave them available for later use. Comments can even act as notifications and reminders in your HTML. In alignment with good practice, we add comments into our HTML code, especially in complex documents, to indicate sections of a document. This will help us and others to better understand the code and increase its readability.

We can create an HTML comment using the character sequence `<!--` to mark the start of the comment, and the character sequence `-->` to mark the end of the comment. When parsing the document, the web browser will automatically ignore everything placed between these two markers, regardless of whether it is plain content or HTML markup. The following example puts an HTML comment before the Education section.

```
<hr>
<!-- Starting Education section-->
<h2>Education</h2>
```

We can place our comments in multiple lines as long as <!-- is placed before the first line and --> is placed after the last line. However, the double-dash sequence "--" may not appear inside a comment except as part of the closing --> tag. This prevents comment nesting, as a comment cannot be nested inside another comment without the double-dash. Additionally, we must make sure that there are no spaces in the start-of-comment string between '<' and '!', meaning that < !-- will not be rendered properly. For example **(Figure 17)**, if we comment out the list in the Portfolio section in the final document, the browser will only display the paragraph text.

```
<h2 id="portfolio">Portfolio</h2>
<p>I have worked as a freelance web designer for the
following companies</p>
<!--
<ul>
    <li>H<sub>2</sub>O Wireless - a broadband Internet
provider</li>
    <li>DSQUARED<sup>2</sup> - an international
fashion house</li>
</ul>
-->
```

Fg. 17 : Invisible commented list.

Wrapping Things Up

There are a lot more tags and attributes in the HTML5 specification, but the content in this book is sufficient for starters. The purpose of any type of markup is to add meaning to a document; we can even think of going through a book with a highlighter pen as adding markup to a document. As it was mentioned previously, when HTML first appeared, the purpose of markup was to explain the structure of a document—what text represents a heading, what is a paragraph, what is a bulleted point, and so on. As it grew in popularity, HTML started to include markup that controlled the appearance of documents. HTML5 aims to return the markup function to solely describing the structure and semantics of the document.

Almost all HTML elements are interpreted by web browsers and presented in a different manner from each other. For example, the <h1> to <h6> elements are all presented differently from the content of a <p> element; list items in an <ol> element are presented differently from those in a <ul> element. However, all of these elements describe the structure of the document: what is a heading, what is an item in a numbered list, and so on. The way the content of these elements is presented reflects the structure that the markup imposes, which is why the heading elements get smaller from <h1> through to <h6>, and why the <li> elements create separate numbered items or bulleted points depending on whether they are contained inside an <ol> or <ul> element.

Elements that describe a document's structure are very different from those that just affect the presentation of the document without adding any meaning. Therefore, HTML5 cuts these purely presentational elements and attributes from HTML.

| 4 |
Content Structure

HTML5 is all about the semantics. Semantic elements add meaning and structure to the content of our pages by letting us identify the logical purpose of its different areas.

Before defining the specifications, HTML5 contributors analyzed existing web pages to determine their common elements. Consequently, HTML5 now includes new elements that are solely used to define meaning and structure. These elements are used for grouping related content together, defining which parts of the content are header, footer or main body elements, describing navigational menus, etc. The website user is never aware of this information, but many tools use it. For example, search engines use the semantic elements to learn more about our page. Screen reading programs present the content more effectively, as semantic elements create more accessible content. Other tools can be used to extract data from our page and use it in a variety of different ways, like presenting it in a newsfeed.

Sectioning Content

Sectioning content is used to divide an HTML document into sections. Every section of the document would generally have its own header, main content and possibly footer.

In HTML revisions prior to HTML5, more notably HTML 4 and XHTML 1, the choices for sectioning content were rather limited. The only sectioning elements designers had to work with were the <body> and <div> tags; <div> is a generic element used to signify a division. This made the ***semantic markup*** of a document virtually impossible and made it difficult for screen readers and other assistive devices to evaluate a page. The new HTML5 semantic markup makes it easy for machines and people alike to understand the content's meaning and context and provides a way to differentiate the key content from sidebars or unrelated information.

Each semantic element of HTML5 has no specific output, color, or design... Unless

> **NOTE**
>
> Theoretically, sectioning elements allow us to create document outlines using headings, form titles, table titles, and any other appropriate landmarks that map out the document. The outlining algorithm has been clearly defined in the HTML5 spec, but browsers and assistive technologies have not yet implemented it.

it has been styled with CSS, each semantic element will be invisible, and its contents will appear drab and monotone when viewed in a web browser.

The <section> and <article> Elements

The <section> element is the most generic element for sectioning content and is primarily used for grouping content with similar meanings. It is meant as a general container element with some additional semantic meaning when the content has to represent a logical group of related content. A section, in this context, is a thematic grouping of content, typically starting with its own heading. Additionally, you can use <section> to define page segments. For example, on your web page, you could put blog posts, news, and a sidebar of ads into separate <section> elements.

Similar to <section>, the <article> element was introduced as a way to group together related information in a document. It is most appropriate to consider the <article> element as a specialized type of <section> with more specific semantic meaning. This element represents whatever we consider an article, meaning a section of self-contained content like a newspaper article, blog entry, forum post or similar content items. For example, an <article> element will contain a single blog post, while a <section> element can contain several (or all) blog posts on the page.

What is the actual difference between <section> and <article> elements? A <section> is a logical part of a document, and an <article> is actual content. Think of a newspaper. A <section> element is like the sports section. The sports section has many articles, just like <section> can contain a lot of <article> elements. Semantically, articles may be long and content-rich with the need to be divided into their own bunch of sections. Following are a few examples that show the interchangeable use of <section> and <article>.

A simple web blog article would have the following structure:

```
<article>
    <h1>Blog Article Heading</h1>
    <p>Article Content</p>
</article>
```

Conversely, a page that lists multiple blog articles would have the following structure:

```
<section>
    <article>
    <h1>Blog Article #1 Heading</h1>
    <p>Article Content</p>
    < /article>
 <article>
    <h1>Blog Article #2 Heading</h1>
    <p>Article Content</p>
    < /article>    <article>
    <h1>Blog Article #3 Heading</h1>
    <p>Article Content</p>
< /article>
</section>
```

On the other hand, a long article, like our sample CV, can contain subsections and follow this structure:

```
<article>
    <h1>Curriculum Vitae</h1>
    <section>
    <h2>Personal Info</h2>
    <p>Content</p>
    </section>
    <section>
    <h2>Education</h2>
    <p>Content</p>
    </section>
    <section>
    <h2>Skills</h2>
    <p>Content</p>
    </section>
    <section>
    <h2>Portfolio</h2>
    <p>Content</p>
    </section>
</article>
```

Navigation & Supplemental Content

The <nav> element defines a section of a page that contains navigation links. These links may point to topics on the current page or to other web pages on a website. It is not unusual to have a page with multiple <nav> sections, one for the main navigation menu, one for the submenu, another for topics within the current article, etc. All of the links on a web page don't need to be included inside a <nav> element. Generally speaking, the <nav> element is reserved for the more important navigational sections.

In our sample CV we can use the <nav> element to wrap the initial navigation menu that bookmarks different sections of the CV.

```
<nav>
   <p><a href="#personal">Personal Information</a></p>
   <p><a href="#education">Education</a></p>
   <p><a href="#skills">Skills</a></p>
   <p><a href="#portfolio">Portfolio</a></p>
</nav>
```

The <aside> element is perfectly suited for a sidebar. A sidebar can refer to a bar physically located to the side of a page or a section of content that provides "additional information." Essentially, <aside> represents a complete chunk of content that's separate from the main content of the page but is still related to that content. For example, it makes sense to use <aside> to create a sidebar with related content or links next to a main article. We can also use <aside> to define a block of ads.

what is this <div> element?

Documents written prior to the advent of HTML5 are plagued with <div> tags. The <div> tag was the king element of semantic markup in previous HTML revisions. It was the only container available for sectioning off content, but it was far more appropriate for defining web page layout than tables. In combination with CSS styles used through IDs and classes, the <div> element allowed us to create visually rich pages with a rather flexible design. In HTML5, <div> has the semantic meaning of a general element. As modern HTML coding requires us to use the most suitable or semantically accurate element, the <div> element is now used only when there are no other elements that are more appropriate.

Headers & Footers

The <header> element groups together introductory content that may also include navigational links. The <header> usually wraps the heading section of a website including the logo, tagline, and navigation menu. It can also appear at the beginning of an article and include content such as a title, a byline and maybe some links to article subtopics. Traditionally, when we think of a header, we imagine only one header per page. In an HTML5 document we can have more than one <header> section as long as each <header> section relates to different content.

For example, in our sample CV we can include the Curriculum Vitae heading, the image and the navigation menu in a <header> element.

```
<header>
    <h1>Curriculum Vitae</h1>
    <p><img src="images\cv_picture.jpg" alt="Scott Johnson profile picture" width="100" height ="150"></p>
    <nav>
        <p><a href="#personal">Personal Information</a></p>
        <p><a href="#education">Education</a></p>
        <p><a href="#skills">Skills</a></p>
        <p><a href="#portfolio">Portfolio</a></p>
    </nav>
</header>
```

The <footer> element defines a footer at the bottom of the page or the section. A <footer> typically contains information such as copyright, contact, sitemap, related documents and similar items. Just like with the <header> element, we may have multiple <footer> elements per page, each grouped into a different <section>.

Semantic Images with <figure> & <figcaption>

The ability to add images on the web influenced the growth of the WWW from academia to a worldwide wonder. The <img> element has existed since the early days of the World Wide Web. From a semantic perspective, the <img> element is greatly limited when it comes to associating explanatory text with the image. While the 'alt' attribute does partially deal with this issue, this text is neither visible nor functional beyond its accessibility features.

To address this issue, HTML5 offers the <figure> and <figcaption> elements. The <figure> element groups the figure with its corresponding caption. For example, we can use the <figure> and <figcaption> to add greater semantic meaning to the image in our sample CV.

```
<figure>
   <img src="images\cv_picture.jpg"
alt="Scott Johnson's profile picture"
width="100" height ="150">
   <figcaption>Scott Johnson</figcaption>
</figure>
```

Physically, the figure itself does not necessarily have to be an <img> element. It can be an SVG drawing, a <canvas> element or even an ASCII graphic, generally anything that can be interpreted as a figure.

> **NOTE**
>
> The <group> element was a new HTML5 element used to combine multiple heading levels such as a title and a subtitle. However, this element has been dropped since it was "fraught with accessibility problems and lacked many compelling use cases."

> **NOTE**
>
> The <canvas> element is a new HTML5 element that acts as a container for graphics. The graphics themselves are created or drawn via scripting, and the practical application of this element goes beyond the scope of this book.

HTML5 Compatibility

When using the HTML5 elements described in this book, it is necessary to acknowledge that older browsers, like IE8, lack the capability to recognize these elements. When browsers can't recognize a specific tag, they simply ignore the tag and render the remaining content as simple text. This is acceptable up to a certain point, as semantic elements are not meant for formatting, but ignoring tags means that the browser will not structure the text in a separate line and will treat everything as part of the same element. In addition to not representing unrecognized elements, IE doesn't even acknowledge their existence, thus preventing us from styling these elements with CSS.

To resolve this issue we will have to trick the older IE browser into recognizing a foreign element by registering it with a JavaScript command. As JavaScript is beyond the scope of this book and beyond the scope of many web designers, we will have to resort to a strategy called *HTML5 Shiv*. HTML5 Shiv is an already created fully compatible JavaScript code developed by Sjoerd Visscher and is available online via googlecode.com. We don't have to retrieve or understand this code to use it. Rather, we simply need to reference it in the head section of our page like this:

```
<head>
    <meta charset="utf-8">
    <title>Curriculum Vitae</title>
    <script src="http://html5shiv.googlecode.com/svn/trunk/html5.js">
    </script>
</head>
```

When we want to add JavaScript code to our web page, we use the `<script>` element. In the example above, by using the src attribute, this element grabs the html5.js JavaScript file from the web server at html5shiv.googlecode.com and runs it before the browser starts processing the rest of the page, thus rendering any HTML elements properly. The *script* is short, simple, loads very fast and uses code to create all the new HTML5 elements for older browsers. Then, all we have to do is use the new elements and style them with appropriate CSS rules.

Technically, we can solve most HTML5 issues of older, non-IE browsers with CSS rules. Therefore, if we only want the HTML5 Shiv JavaScript code executed for IE browsers, we can place it inside a conditional comment. A ***conditional comment*** is a special type of comment that only Internet Explorer can read; it can even target specific versions of IE.

```
<head>
    <meta charset="utf-8">
    <title>Curriculum Vitae</title>
    <!--[if lt IE 9]>
        <script src="http://html5shiv.googlecode.com/svn/trunk/html5.js">
        </script>
    <![endif]-->
</head>
```

confirm a website for html5 compliance

To verify how well a website supports HTML5, we can use an HTML5 validator tool. There are many online tools available, but the one that conforms to the most recent HTML5 specifications is the W3C Markup Validation Service available at http://validator.w3.org. The W3C Markup Validation Service enables us to verify a website against non-English character-encoding types and even older markup languages, such as HTML versions 4.01, 3.2, and 2.0, various XHTML standards, MathML, Scalable Vector Graphics (SVG), and Synchronized Multimedia Integration Language (SMIL).

To use the W3C Markup Validation Service, the web page to be tested has to be published online. To use this tool, we submit the URL address of the web page, and the tool downloads the HTML source code for the site, auto-detects the encoding and document type, and analyzes the page for compliance. The registered infractions are categorized like errors and warnings and are rated by severity. The tool even offers explanations and possible solutions to the noted problems.

Even if an HTML5 web page fails validation, it may still render correctly in a web browser. This is because the HTML5 specifications state that web developers must avoid deprecated tags, but web browsers may honor them. This is a critical requirement of maintaining backward compatibility with earlier HTML versions and web pages that have not been updated to the latest standard.

With all of the interventions thus far, our sample CV should now have the following HTML structure:

```
<!DOCTYPE html>
<html>
<head>
    <meta charset="utf-8">
    <title>Curriculum Vitae</title>
    <!--[if lt IE 9]>
        <script src="http://html5shiv.googlecode.com/svn/trunk/html5.js">
        </script>
    <![endif]-->
</head>
<body>
<article>
<header>
    <h1>Curriculum Vitae</h1>
    <figure>
        <img src="images\cv_picture.jpg" alt="Scott Johnson's profile picture" width="100" height ="150">
        <figcaption>Scott Johnson</figcaption>
    </figure>
    <nav>
        <p><a href="#personal">Personal Information</a></p>
        <p><a href="#education">Education</a></p>
        <p><a href="#skills">Skills</a></p>
        <p><a href="#portfolio">Portfolio</a></p>
    </nav>
</header>
<section>
    <h2 id="personal">Personal Info</h2>
```

HTML QUICKSTART GUIDE

```html
    <p><strong>Name:</strong> Scott Johnson</p>
    <p><strong>Occupation:</strong> Web Designer</p>
    <p><strong>Date of birth: </strong> 09/09/1980</p>
    <p><strong>Address:</strong> <br>
    523 Beaumont Way<br>
    Santa Rosa<br>
    California 52409</p>
</section>
<hr>
<section>
    <h2>Education</h2>
    <ul>
        <li>MIT</li>
            <ul>
                <li>PhD Degree in Computer Science</li>
                <li>Bachelor Degree in Computer Science</li>
            </ul>
        <li>Santa Rosa High School</li>
    </ul>
</section>
    <hr>
<section>
    <h2 id="skills">Skills</h2>
    <table>
    <tr>
        <th>Web Technology</th>
        <th>Skill Level</th>
    </tr>
    <tr>
        <td>HTML</td>
        <td>Expert</td>
    </tr>
```

```html
        <tr>
           <td>CSS</td>
           <td>Expert</td>
        </tr>
        <tr>
           <td>JavaScript</td>
           <td>Advanced</td>
        </tr>
        </table>
</section>
<hr>
<section>
   <h2 id="portfolio">Portfolio</h2>
   <p>I have worked as a freelance web designer for the following companies:</p>
   <ul>
       <li>H<sub>2</sub>O Wireless - a broadband Internet provider</li>
       <li>DSQUARED<sup>2</sup> - an international fashion house</li>
   </ul>
</section>
</article>
</body>
</html>
```

summary

This book covered a wide array of topics, but they all dealt with how to get information from a database. Initially, we were introduced to SQL, the language for communicating with a database. The focus was on using SQL as a query language, while the other aspects of the language were omitted.

We learned that the key to extracting data with SQL is the SELECT statement, which allows us to select the columns and tables from which to extract data. We now know how to filter with the WHERE clause by specifying any number of conditions in order to obtain the results that suit our particular needs. We were introduced to logical and comparison operators in order to better manage situational data conditions. We also learned how to manage the order of results in ascending or descending order, based on one or more columns with the ORDER BY clause.

By using the JOIN statements we tackled the slightly tricky topic of selecting data from more than one table. We managed to link two or more tables to form a new results set, and we learned the importance of the unknown (NULL) value.

We then summarized and aggregated data rather than getting results based on individual records. Central to this concept was the GROUP BY statement, which enables results to be based on groups of common data. In conjunction with SQL's aggregate functions such as COUNT, SUM, AVG, MAX, and MIN we learned how to manipulate data and calculate specific values. We also explored the HAVING clause, which filters out the result of groups using various conditions, much like a WHERE clause does for a SELECT statement. Conversely, we learned how to add new records to a database using the INSERT INTO statement, updated already existing data with the UPDATE statement, and learned about the DELETE statement, which allows us to delete all or specific records from a table.

Finally, we learned how to use SQL to define the structure of the database itself. We used the CREATE DATABASE statement to create a new database from scratch.

We also learned about CREATE/ALTER/DROP TABLE commands to successfully manipulate the structures of tables.

glossary

Accessibility -
The ability of people with disabilities to use a website, including the visually impaired, hearing impaired, colorblind users, or those with other disabilities.

Anchor -
The text a link uses to refer to our site.

Browser -
The program that enables a user to view our web site.

Cascading Style Sheets (CSS)-
Rules that define a website's look and feel.

Comment -
A bit of information contained in the HTML code which the browser ignores.

Conditional Comment -
A special type of comment visible only to Internet Explorer browsers.

Deprecated -
Code that is no longer included in the language specifications.

Doctype -
A declaration that specifies which version of HTML is used in a web page.

Element -
The central building block of any HTML document.

Extensible Markup Language (XML) -
A markup language used for writing custom markup languages.

HTML5 Shiv -
A fully compatible JavaScript code that recreates all of the new HTML5 elements for compatibility with older browsers.

Hypertext Markup Language (HTML) -
The primary language used for writing web pages.

Hypertext -
Any computer text that includes hyperlinks.

Metadata -
The data contained in the head of the web page that offers additional information about that web page.

Non-Breaking Space -
A white-space character that isn't condensed by HTML.

Script -

A portion of code, most often written in JavaScript, that makes the page more dynamic and interactive.

Semantic Markup -

Markup that offers context to what the content contains.

Tag -

A set of markup characters used around an element to indicate where it begins and where it ends.

Web Page -

A single document written in HTML meant to be viewed in a web browse.

about clydebank

We are a multi-media publishing company that provides reliable, high-quality and easily accessible information to a global customer base. Developed out of the need for beginner-friendly content that is accessible across multiple formats, we deliver reliable, up-to-date, high-quality information through our multiple product offerings.

Through our strategic partnerships with some of the world's largest retailers, we are able to simplify the learning process for customers around the world, providing them with an authoritative source of information for the subjects that matter to them. Our end-user focused philosophy puts the satisfaction of our customers at the forefront of our mission. We are committed to creating multi-media products that allow our customers to learn what they want, when they want and how they want.

ClydeBank Technology is a division of the multimedia-publishing firm ClydeBank Media LLC. ClydeBank Media's goal is to provide affordable, accessible information to a global market through different forms of media such as eBooks, paperback books and audio books. Company divisions are based on subject matter, each consisting of a dedicated team of researchers, writers, editors and designers.

For more information, please visit us at :
www.clydebankmedia.com
or contact *info@clydebankmedia.com*

Your world, simplified.

notes

How Being A ClydeBank Media VIP is a Win-Win for Everyone

ClydeBank Media Publishes Book
- PAPERBACK
- KINDLE
- AUDIOBOOK

VIP Member Receives Free Copy

VIP MEMBER

VIP Member Leaves Valuable Feedback

ClydeBank Media Learns From Feedback

VIP Member Educates Future Customer

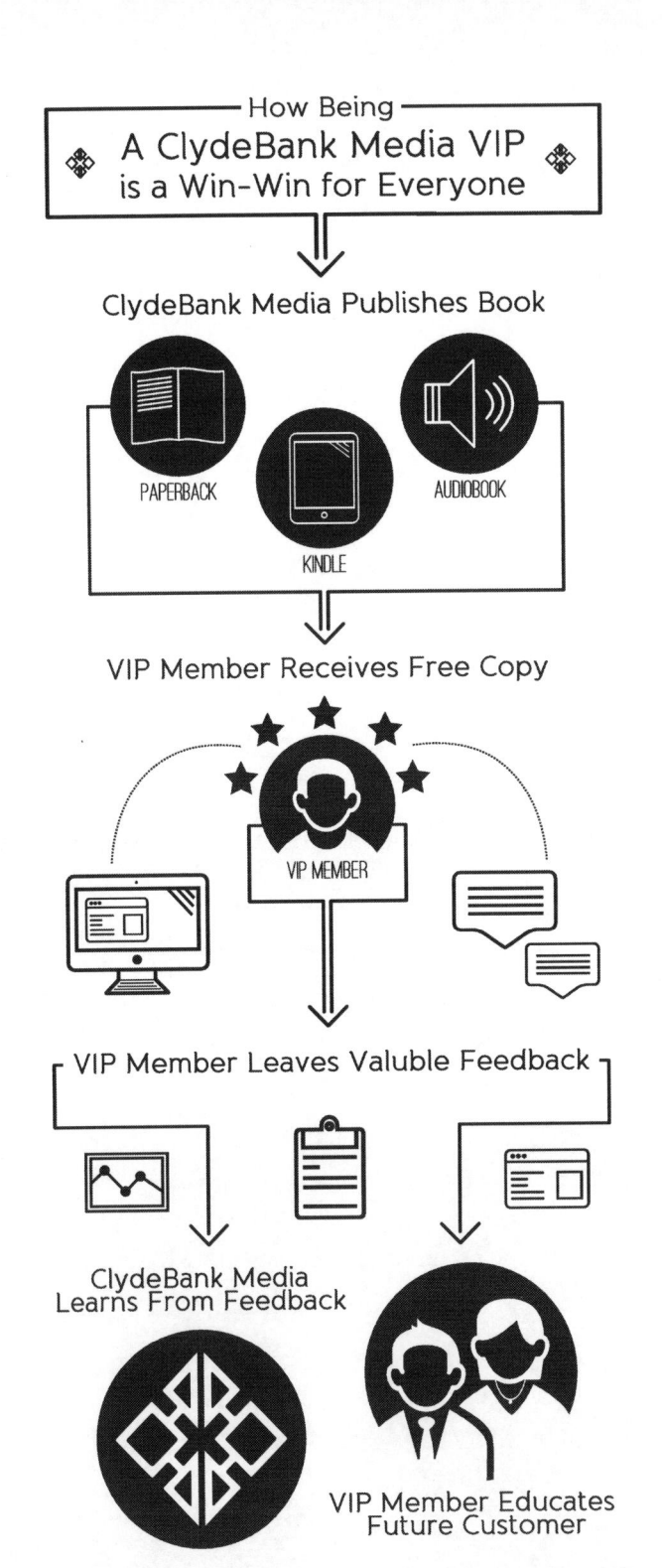

Visit *www.clydebankmedia.com/vip* to find out more and become a VIP member!

Get a *FREE* ClydeBank Media Audiobook + 30 Day Free Trial to Audible.com

Get titles like this absolutely free :

- Business Plan Quickstart Guide
- Options Trading Quickstart Guide
- ITIL For Beginners
- Scrum Quickstart Guide
- JavaScript Quickstart Guide
- 3D Printing Quickstart Guide

- LLC Quickstart Guide
- Lean Six Sigma Quickstart Guide
- Project Management QuickStart Guide
- Social Security Simplified
- Medicare Simplified
- and more!

To Sign Up & Get your Free Audiobook, visit :
www.clydebankmedia.com/audible-trial

Made in the USA
Middletown, DE
24 July 2016